ART DECO ARCHITECTURE
MIAMI BEACH

"POST OFFICE"

© pauiclemence.com

published by SCHIFFERBOOKS.COM

ART DECO ARCHITECTURE
MIAMI BEACH

"CARLYLE"

published by SCHIFFERBOOKS.COM

ART DECO ARCHITECTURE
MIAMI BEACH

"ESSEX HOUSE"

published by SCHIFFERBOOKS.COM

ART DECO ARCHITECTURE
MIAMI BEACH

"SHELBORNE"

published by SCHIFFERBOOKS.COM

© paulclemence.com

ART DECO ARCHITECTURE
MIAMI BEACH

"DELANO"

published by SCHIFFERBOOKS.COM

©paulclemence.com

ART DECO ARCHITECTURE
MIAMI BEACH

"WARSAW"

published by SCHIFFERBOOKS.COM

© paulclemence.com

ART DECO ARCHITECTURE
MIAMI BEACH

"WALDORF"

© paulclemence.com

published by SCHIFFERBOOKS.COM

ART DECO ARCHITECTURE
MIAMI BEACH

"RITZ II"

published by SCHIFFERBOOKS.COM

ART DECO ARCHITECTURE
MIAMI BEACH

"FOUR"

published by SCHIFFERBOOKS.COM

© paulclemence.com

ART DECO ARCHITECTURE
MIAMI BEACH

"PIGEON"

published by SCHIFFERBOOKS.COM

ART DECO ARCHITECTURE
MIAMI BEACH

"CUBIST"

published by SCHIFFERBOOKS.COM

ART DECO ARCHITECTURE
MIAMI BEACH

"DECO WINDOW"

published by SCHIFFERBOOKS.COM

© paulclemence.com

ART DECO ARCHITECTURE
MIAMI BEACH

"LIGHT CARVING"

published by SCHIFFERBOOKS.COM

© paulclemence.com

ART DECO ARCHITECTURE
MIAMI BEACH

"BREAKWATER"

© paulclemence.com

published by SCHIFFERBOOKS.COM

ART DECO ARCHITECTURE
MIAMI BEACH

"ALBION"

© paulclemence.com

published by SCHIFFERBOOKS.COM

ART DECO ARCHITECTURE
MIAMI BEACH

"LOEWS"

published by SCHIFFERBOOKS.COM

© paulclemence.com

ART DECO ARCHITECTURE
MIAMI BEACH

"NETHERLAND/BELOW"

published by SCHIFFERBOOKS.COM

© paulclemence.com

ART DECO ARCHITECTURE
MIAMI BEACH

"EYEBROWS + TURRET"

published by SCHIFFERBOOKS.COM

© paulclemence.com

ART DECO ARCHITECTURE
MIAMI BEACH

"WORKER"

published by SCHIFFERBOOKS.COM

ART DECO ARCHITECTURE
MIAMI BEACH

"NEON OCEAN DR."

© paulclemence.com

published by SCHIFFERBOOKS.COM